W9-BER-854

Presented to

_____

From

_____

Date

_____

FAMILY TRADITIONS
1835 W. Capitol Dr.
Appleton, WI 54914
Ph. 920-733-5391 / Fax 920-993-9968
E-mail: familytrad@aol.com

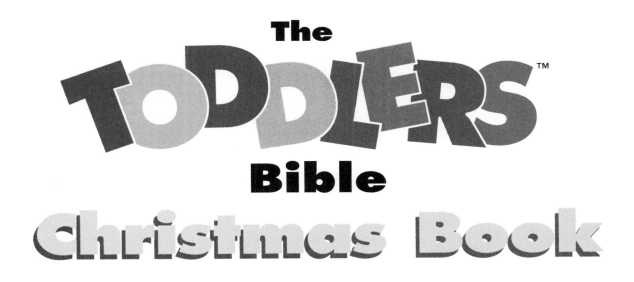

The Toddlers Bible Christmas Book

V. Gilbert Beers

Illustrated by
Carol Boerke

VICTOR BOOKS

A DIVISION OF SCRIPTURE PRESS PUBLICATIONS INC.
USA CANADA ENGLAND

Copyright © 1995 by Educational Publishing Concepts, Inc. Wheaton, Illinois

Text © 1992 by V. Gilbert Beers

All rights reserved. Written permission must be secured from the publisher to use or reproduce any part of this book, except for brief quotations in critical reviews or articles.

Published in Wheaton, Illinois by Victor Books/Scripture Press.

ISBN 1-56476-527-X

Printed in the United States of America

1 2 3 4 5 6 — 02 01 00 99 98 97 96 95

CONTENTS

An Angel Brings Good News

Have you ever seen an angel? Mary did.
The angel talked to her. He told her
some good news.

"You will have a baby," the angel said. "He will be God's Son. You will call Him Jesus."

"I will do what God wants me to do,"
said Mary.

Then the angel was gone. Do you think
Mary thanked God for His good news?

Baby Jesus

Shhh. Do you see the baby? This is
Baby Jesus.

Shhh. Do you see the animals? Baby Jesus is sleeping in a manger.

Shhh. The people of Bethlehem are asleep
now. They do not know that this is
God's Son.

Shhh. Whisper a prayer to God now.
"Thank You, God, for sending Baby Jesus."

Shepherds Visit Jesus

"Look! Is that an angel?" a shepherd asked.
There WAS an angel in the sky.

The angel talked to the shepherd and his friends. "Good news! God's Son has been born in Bethlehem!"

17

The sky was filled with angels. They sang
and praised God. Then they were gone.

The shepherds hurried to Bethlehem to see Baby Jesus. Would you like to have been there too?

Wise Men Visit Jesus

"We must follow the star," a Wise Man said.
"Now," said the others.

The Wise Men rode camels far from home.
They went all the way to Bethlehem.

"This is the place," they said.
"The new King is here!"

The Wise Men gave wonderful gifts to little
Jesus. That made them very happy.

Going to Egypt

Could anyone not like little Jesus? Yes. A bad king did not like Him. He wanted to kill Jesus.

This bad king had soldiers. "Kill Him!" the king said. So the soldiers looked for little Jesus

But an angel talked to Joseph. "Take little
Jesus to Egypt," the angel said.

So little Jesus lived in Egypt for a while.
God took care of Him there.

TIPS FOR PARENTS

As you read these stories to your toddler, point out the characters as they appear in a Nativity scene you might have in your home.

Turn to the passage listed for each story in your Bible. As you read the story to your toddler, show that these stories of Jesus' birth are in your big Bible, too.

An Angel Brings Good News—Luke 1:26–38

Baby Jesus—Luke 2:1–7

Shepherds Visit Jesus—Luke 2:8–20

Wise Men Visit Jesus—Matthew 2:1–12

Going to Egypt—Matthew 2:13–18

Something Special To Do With Your Toddler

Say something like, "The story of the Wise Men is a story of giving to Jesus. They gave Him three special gifts. What can we give Him as special gifts?"

Make a mobile or picture to hang on the wall using a picture of a heart, a coin, and a clock. You may want to cut these from construction paper or find the pictures in old magazines.

Explain that the heart represents our *love*, the coin represents our *money* and *things*, and the clock represents our *time* and *talents*.

Sing the song, "Twinkle, Twinkle, Little Star" together to remember the special star that told of Jesus' birth.

"Talk About It" Questions

1. What did the angel say to Mary?

2. Why is Baby Jesus so special?

3. Where did the shepherds go? Who told them to go there?

4. What did the Wise Men give Jesus?

5. Who took care of Baby Jesus?

6. What can you give to Jesus? Will you thank God for sending His Son?